PRIMARY SOURCES IN AMERICAN HISTORY™

THE LOUISIANA PURCHASE
A PRIMARY SOURCE HISTORY OF JEFFERSON'S LANDMARK PURCHASE FROM NAPOLÉON

JAN GOLDBERG

rosen central
Primary Source™

The Rosen Publishing Group, Inc., New York

Published in 2004 by The Rosen Publishing Group, Inc.
29 East 21st Street, New York, NY 10010

First Edition

Library of Congress Cataloging-in-Publication Data

Goldberg, Jan.
The Louisiana Purchase: a primary source history of Jefferson's landmark purchase from Napoléon / Jan Goldberg.—1st ed.
    p. cm. — (Primary sources in American history)
Summary: Primary sources describe the history of the Louisiana Purchase, from Jefferson's dream of expansion and his negotiations with Napoléon for the land to the exploration of the new territory by Lewis and Clark.
ISBN 0-8239-4006-3 (library binding)
1. Louisiana Purchase—Sources—Juvenile literature. [1. Louisiana Purchase—Sources.] I. Title. II. Series.
E333.G655 2004
973.4'6—dc21

2003001080

Manufactured in the United States of America

On the front cover: *Traite avec les Etats Unis*, a lithograph based on a painting by F. Adam from the late nineteenth century. Courtesy of the Louisiana State Museum.

On the back cover: First row (left to right): immigrants arriving at Ellis Island; Generals Lee and Grant meet to discuss terms of Confederate surrender at Appomattox, Virginia. Second row (left to right): Lewis and Clark meeting with a western Indian tribe during the expedition of the Corps of Discovery; Napoleon at the signing of the Louisiana Purchase Treaty. Third row (left to right): Cherokees traveling along the Trail of Tears during their forced relocation west of the Mississippi River; escaped slaves traveling on the Underground Railroad.

CONTENTS

80.442

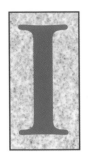

INTRODUCTION

Thomas Jefferson, the third president of the United States, was one of the most talented men of all time. A man of unusual distinction in American and world history, Jefferson was a political leader, a scientist, a writer, an inventor, an architect, and perhaps most important of all, a visionary.

Jefferson had always dreamed that one day the United States would stretch from the Atlantic Ocean to the Pacific Ocean. When he was sworn into office in 1801, however, the western boundary of the United States extended only as far as the Mississippi River. Beyond this great body of water lay an immense expanse of land known as the Louisiana Territory. In this uncharted wilderness, Jefferson felt, lay America's future.

AN AMERICAN DREAMER

Hoping to acquire this land in order to insure the young country's continuing strength, security, and prosperity, Jefferson encountered several obstacles to his dream of westward expansion. The most important of these was that the land was being passed back and forth between France and Spain, held hostage by the political and military strategies of the old European powers.

Though the chances of gaining possession of the Louisiana Territory seemed dim in 1802, when Jefferson sent his representatives to France to try to purchase the city of New Orleans, the political situation in the New World and Europe was rapidly

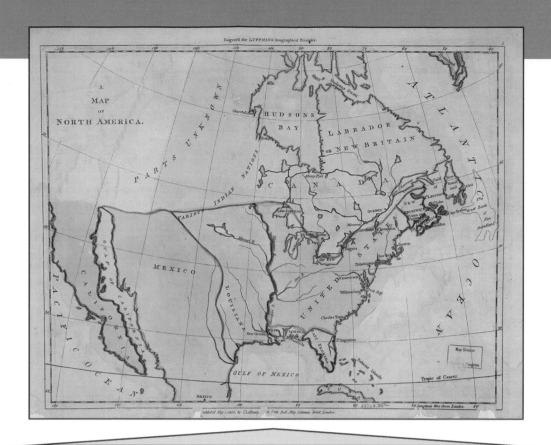

This 1803 map of North America was created by John Luffman. Though highly inaccurate, this map gives a sense of the size and extent of the Louisiana Territory (the map's pink central portion). Following the Louisiana Purchase, Thomas Jefferson would organize an expedition—led by Meriwether Lewis and William Clark—to explore the new territory. One of the end results of this trip was the creation of a far more accurate and detailed map of North America.

changing. By April 1803, France had offered to sell not only New Orleans but the entire Louisiana Territory to the United States. Jumping at the unexpected offer, the United States purchased the 828,000-square-mile (2,145,000-square-kilometer) territory for $15 million, or less than three cents an acre.

This is the story of the Louisiana Purchase, often referred to as the greatest real estate deal in history, one that would instantly double the size of the United States and forever alter the country's sense of itself. If America is the land of opportunity, a vast and free land stretching from sea to shining sea, this is largely due to the vision of Thomas Jefferson—a vision as expansive and soaring as the nation he helped build.

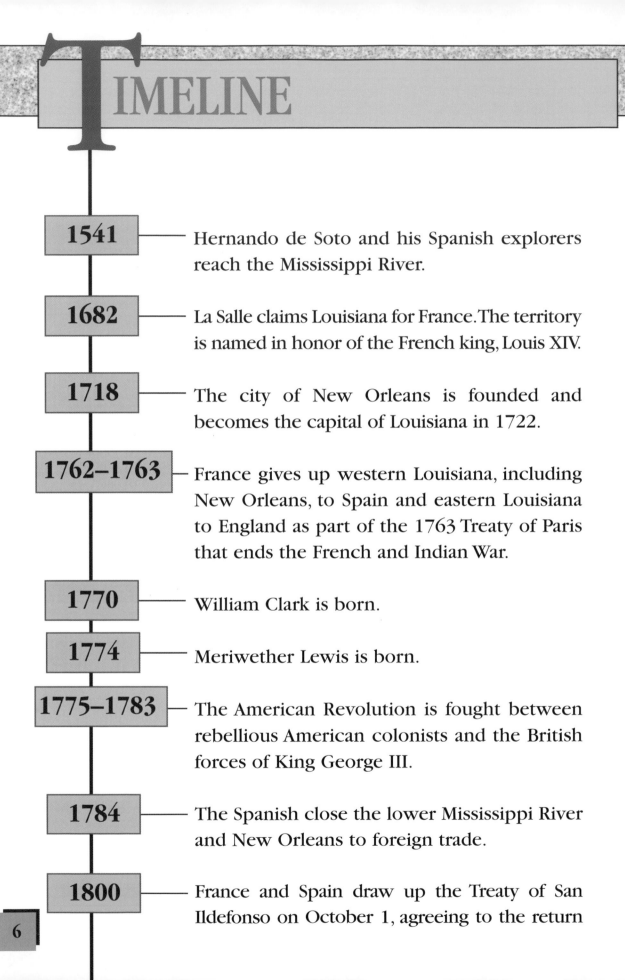

TIMELINE

1541 — Hernando de Soto and his Spanish explorers reach the Mississippi River.

1682 — La Salle claims Louisiana for France. The territory is named in honor of the French king, Louis XIV.

1718 — The city of New Orleans is founded and becomes the capital of Louisiana in 1722.

1762–1763 — France gives up western Louisiana, including New Orleans, to Spain and eastern Louisiana to England as part of the 1763 Treaty of Paris that ends the French and Indian War.

1770 — William Clark is born.

1774 — Meriwether Lewis is born.

1775–1783 — The American Revolution is fought between rebellious American colonists and the British forces of King George III.

1784 — The Spanish close the lower Mississippi River and New Orleans to foreign trade.

1800 — France and Spain draw up the Treaty of San Ildefonso on October 1, agreeing to the return

TIMELINE

of western Louisiana and New Orleans to France.

1801 —— Thomas Jefferson becomes the third president of the United States.

1803 —— France sells Louisiana and the Mississippi River valley to the United States in the Louisiana Purchase.

1804–1806 — Lewis and Clark explore the Louisiana Territory.

1804 —— Congress divides the Louisiana Territory to make it easier to govern. The southern section of the territory becomes the Territory of Orleans. The northern section becomes the District of Louisiana.

1805 —— The Territory of Orleans and the District of Louisiana are reorganized as the Territory of Louisiana.

1812 —— Louisiana becomes the eighteenth state.

1819 —— The United States acquires East and West Florida from Spain.

CHAPTER 1

LOUISIANA UNDER THE FRENCH AND SPANISH

The land that would come to be known as the Louisiana Territory was claimed for France on April 9, 1682, by René-Robert Cavelier, Sieur de La Salle (*sieur* is the French word for "sire" or "lord"). He chose to name the new territory Louisiana in honor of the French king then on the throne, Louis XIV. La Salle and his band of explorers had just completed a three-month expedition down the Mississippi River to the Gulf of Mexico, becoming the first Europeans to discover the large delta where the river ended. La Salle marked that spot with a cross and a wooden column that displayed the French coat of arms. This was the first official European claim to the land that was now called the Louisiana Territory.

The French Stake a Claim

The first contact Europeans had with the Mississippi River came when the Spanish explorer Hernando de Soto "discovered" it in 1541. The region had been explored by Spanish conquistadors more than a century before its "discovery" by the French. Yet Spain had never established any colonies there, finding the climate, geography, and wildlife too harsh for prolonged settlement. Instead, the Spanish focused their

The Spanish explorer Hernando de Soto and a 600-man army landed on the southwestern coast of Florida in 1539 with the goal of claiming the area for Spain and searching for treasure. On May 8, 1541, they became the first Europeans to discover the Mississippi River, as pictured here in William Henry Powell's *De Soto's Discovery of the Mississippi in 1541*. In his search for treasure—gold, in particular—de Soto was often brutal in his dealings with Native Americans, engaging in many battles with them. Only half of de Soto's men would survive the four-year exploration of the southeastern area of North America. De Soto himself died of fever in 1542.

attention on Mexico, where gold and other precious metals were plentiful.

With no strong Spanish claim to the territory, King Louis XIV became interested in claiming the land in an effort to extend the French Empire into the New World and counter the growing influence of Spain and Britain in the new colonies. French settlers quickly traveled to Louisiana, believing that the land was appropriate for both farming and mining silver and gold. In European eyes, the French were strengthening their claim of ownership of the territory.

The Birth and Growth of New Orleans

New Orleans was founded in 1718 by Jean-Baptiste Le Moyne, Sieur de Bienville, about 100 miles (160 kilometers) upriver from the mouth of the Mississippi. It quickly became an important center of trade, serving as a depot for goods traveling down the river on their way to the Atlantic and the eastern seaboard or Europe. As a result, the city began to attract a large and multiethnic population of traders and merchants, many of whom were former convicts sent over by trading companies. The new city and the territory beyond it attracted people of French, Spanish, Latin American, German, English, and Canadian descent (in addition to African slaves). In fact, the city enjoyed such popularity that it became the capital of Louisiana in 1722. In addition, New Orleans's strategic location allowed it to protect the mouth of the Mississippi River.

Even though many settlers traveled to the Louisiana Territory to establish a new life, the area they chose to live in represented only a very small portion of the total land available. The vast majority of the enormous territory remained unexplored and unknown to almost everyone but Native Americans.

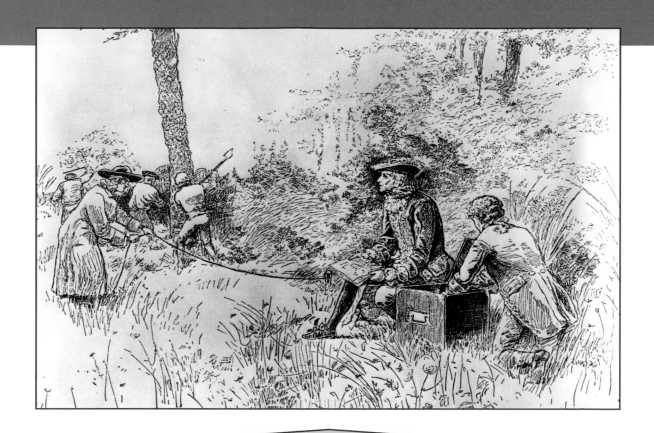

Jean Baptiste Le Moyne, Sieur de Bienville, was the French governor of Louisiana from 1706 to 1726. Bienville's father had emigrated from France to settle in Canada in 1640. Bienville was born in Montreal, Quebec, in 1680. In 1698 and 1699, Bienville accompanied his brother, Iberville, in an expedition sent from France to explore the territory near the mouth of the Mississippi River. They founded a settlement at old Biloxi, where Bienville became commandant and, later, governor of the French colony of Louisiana. In 1718 he selected the site for a new settlement, called New Orleans, which became the seat of government in 1722. In this 1718 engraving by H. Bridgman, Bienville *(seated)* is helping to lay the groundwork for the city of New Orleans.

The French and Indian War

In 1754, two prominent European powers, Great Britain and France, were plunged into a long, serious conflict on North American soil known as the French and Indian War. This war was waged because both countries were fighting for control of the continent. The conflict lasted from 1754 to 1763.

In the end, Great Britain was the war's victor and expected France to hand over all of its territory in North America. In a calculated move before the peace treaty was signed, however, the French king, Louis XV, decided that he would present Louisiana to his cousin, Charles III, the king of Spain. By doing so, he would avoid any obligation to hand over the Louisiana Territory to Great Britain. Even though it won the French and Indian War, therefore, Great Britain took ownership of only Canada and all the land east of the Mississippi River. This was itself a huge territory, but Great Britain had expected to win almost all of North America by gaining the Louisiana Territory from France. Instead, all of France's land holdings west of the Mississippi River, including the city of New Orleans, went to Spain.

King Louis XV found it easy to give away such a huge piece of territory because he did not place much value on the Louisiana Territory. Considering it nothing but a wasteland, he felt he could easily spare it while also seeming to show his appreciation for the help Spain provided him during the French and Indian War. Most important, Louis prevented Great Britain from gaining dominance over the continent.

Charles III and Spanish Louisiana

At first, Charles III was so unimpressed by the Louisiana Territory that he refused King Louis XV's offer. After all, considering the fact that his country lost the Floridas—rich and fertile lands—to England in the process of helping France in its recent war, Charles III did not think the "western wilderness" was fair compensation for such a sizable loss. (Spain would regain the Floridas from 1781 to 1783, during the Revolutionary War.) He was concerned, however, that if he did not accept the gift, Great

Charles III, king of Spain (pictured above left in a portrait by Francisco de Goya), allied his country with France against England in the European Seven Years' War and the French and Indian War fought simultaneously in North America. When France, ruled by King Louis XV (shown above right in a 1748 portrait by Maurice-Quentin de La Tour), lost the French and Indian War, Spain was forced to hand Florida over to England. As repayment for this loss, Louis XV gave the entire Louisiana Territory to Charles III.

Britain might seize it and further increase the size of its empire. In addition, if Britain took ownership of the Louisiana Territory, its soldiers would be situated near Spain's valuable silver mines in Mexico—a potentially dangerous and volatile situation.

Perhaps most important, the Louisiana Territory included New Orleans, a vital port that controlled the traffic and trade on the mighty Mississippi River. This was an extremely attractive and valuable acquisition. Charles III's advisors felt that accepting the gift was ultimately the right thing for Spain to do. The Spanish king decided that he had no choice but to say yes to France's offer.

In 1762, following Charles III's acceptance of Louis XV's offer, France gave the territory known as Louisiana to Spain in a secret agreement. The transfer of the territory to Spain meant that France no longer had control over any land in North America. Despite the growing presence of Great Britain in the New World, the French king seemed unconcerned about France's sudden lack of a presence there.

Putting little value on his latest acquisition, Charles III did not even bother to send any officials or soldiers to establish control of his new land. In fact, French administrators stayed on in their previous roles and performed their usual duties. The settlers were unaware that there had been a change in government for more than two years. Finally, in 1764, a letter acknowledging the shift from French to Spanish rule was sent to the territory's residents.

Most French settlers were violently opposed to this change. In fact, many who lived in New Orleans sent representatives to Paris to express their strong feelings of disapproval. Since no Spanish officials appeared in the newly acquired territory, the settlers felt that their actions had prevented the Spanish from taking power.

Several years after the secret agreement was signed, however, Don Antonio de Ulloa arrived in New Orleans to finally begin Spanish rule of the Louisiana Territory. The response from the settlers—particularly French merchants and officials and German farmers—was to riot in the streets of New Orleans in 1768. Ulloa, fearing for his life, fled from the area at the earliest opportunity. To replace him, the Spanish sent General Alexander O'Reilly, a harsh and severe military governor.

In 1770, much to everyone's relief, a mild-mannered man, Don Luis de Unzaga, took over. The new governor got along well with the French and recruited many of them to help him run the government. So, even though most of the people in Louisiana were of French origin, spoke French, and followed French customs, Unzaga was so highly thought of that the people gradually and peacefully adjusted to living under Spanish rule. While it was Spain that was in charge, French culture prevailed.

The American Revolution

Prior to the American Revolution, Spanish Louisiana's most formidable enemy, Great Britain, was a troubling presence just across the Mississippi. Along the eastern banks of the river, English settlers had built forts, founded towns, and farmed the land, solidifying their dominance there. In fact, Baton Rouge, an important port town located less than 80 miles (129 km) from New Orleans, stood guarded by British military.

British traders established their control of Louisiana's commerce by setting up their main headquarters near New Orleans. British ships laden with furs and produce took to the waters and plied the river, seeking customers for their wares. It seemed as if Britain was finally gaining a foothold in the Louisiana Territory.

Then, in 1775, the thirteen English colonies in North America declared their independence from Great Britain, forming the United States of America and embarking on a war against Europe's strongest empire. To whom could this tiny newborn nation look for help in its fight against the mighty British? And how would the war affect the balance of power in the Louisiana Territory and the world beyond?

Spanish and French Aid for the Colonists

France and Spain were instrumental in helping the United States win its war of independence against England. When the revolution

Hoping to contain the growth and power of the British Empire, France joined the American colonists in their war of independence against England. On October 19, 1781, in Yorktown, Virginia, in what would turn out to be the final major battle of the war, British Major General Charles O'Hara tried to surrender to French General Jean Baptiste Rochambeau *(as shown above)*. As a token of surrender, he offered Rochambeau the sword of his commander, Lord Charles Cornwallis. The French general refused the offer and pointed O'Hara to General George Washington instead, the head of the U.S. army, whom the English forces refused to acknowledge as legitimate.

began in 1775, Louisiana's Spanish governor, Don Luis de Unzaga, received a letter from General Charles Lee seeking help for the rebelling colonies. Lee warned that if England regained control of the colonies, it would then turn its attention to attacking Spain's most precious holdings—Mexico and Cuba. Lee also emphasized that, in return for Spanish help, an independent United States would respect Spanish claims in North America and not invade its territory. Governor Unzaga decided to aid America's rebels secretly, for he feared that if England found out that he was helping them, the British navy would attack New Orleans.

France, too, helped in the colonies' fight for independence, sending ships to attack those owned by the British and providing the colonists with arms and financial support. In addition, France sent thousands of soldiers to fight side by side with the American rebels. France lent its support less out of an interest to regain territory in the New World than to strike a blow against its longtime enemy. Any action that might weaken the influence of the mighty British Empire was very attractive to France.

When the fighting in the American Revolution finally ceased in 1783, Great Britain agreed to give the land between the Mississippi River and the Appalachian Mountains to the United States. Almost immediately, Americans began pouring across the mountains to begin a new life. The Mississippi River and the port of New Orleans would become the settlers' economic lifeline to the East. When access to that lifeline became threatened in 1802, a chain of events was unleashed that would result in the United States's purchase of the Louisiana Territory and its gradual evolution into a world power.

CHAPTER 2

THE LOSS OF NEW ORLEANS

Thomas Jefferson, the tall, freckle-faced man who would grow up to be the third president of the United States, was born in Albemarle County, Virginia, on April 13, 1743. He spent his youth on a large plantation with his family and a number of slaves. His father was a self-made man who became a surveyor and planter and served in Virginia's House of Burgesses (the colony of Virginia's representative assembly). His mother was from one of Virginia's most prominent families.

Jefferson was an exceptional American who went to college, became an accomplished lawyer and writer, and launched his career in public service by becoming very involved in colonial government. Jefferson entered the House of Burgesses in 1769, when he was only twenty-five. He wrote the Declaration of Independence (the document that announced the colonies' determination to split away from their mother country, England) when he was only thirty-three years old and served as minister to France, governor of Virginia, and secretary of state under President George Washington. Finally, in 1801, Jefferson became president of the young nation he helped create.

In addition to his celebrated public life, Jefferson claimed many other accomplishments. He began designing his elegant home, known as Monticello, when he was about twenty-six

Before becoming the third president of the United States, Thomas Jefferson, shown above in an 1805 Rembrandt Peale portrait, served as treaty commissioner and minister to France from 1784 to 1789. During this time, he was able to observe and report on the French Revolution firsthand. He was initially supportive of the French citizens' fight for freedom from royal tyranny, so similar to the Americans' own recent revolution. He believed that in this sense the French were natural friends of America, especially since they shared a common enemy— England. Yet the uncontrolled violence of the French Revolution and the rise of Napoléon Bonaparte as emperor of France caused him to doubt the good intentions of the French in Europe and North America.

years old; conducted the country's first archaeological survey (finding ancient Native American bones); authored a well-known book, *Notes on Virginia*; established an extensive library; founded the University of Virginia; and had six children with his wife, Martha Wayles Skelton. He is also widely believed to have fathered one or more of his slave Sally Heming's children.

Jefferson's Dream of a Greater America

When Jefferson took the oath of office as the third president of the United States on March 4, 1801, the nation was still young and small. It had declared its independence just twenty-five years earlier. Only 5,308,483 people lived within its borders, which enclosed only a fraction of the territory that the United States currently occupies. (The population of the United States in 2002 was 280,562,489.) Stretching from the Atlantic Ocean in the east to the Mississippi River in the west, from the Great Lakes in the north nearly to the Gulf of Mexico in the south (roughly 1,000 miles square, or 1,609 kilometers square), the nation was about a third the size of today's continental United States. Even so, most of this relatively small territory lay untouched and uninhabited by white settlers, with two-thirds of the population living within 50 miles (80 km) of the Atlantic Ocean.

One of Jefferson's exceptional attributes was his visionary mind. He had a unique ability to imagine how things might be in the future, which allowed him to make decisions in the present that would benefit the country in the years to come. In attempting to anticipate the future, he tried to put the country in a position to take best advantage of the likely changes ahead.

Jefferson imagined a rich and powerful United States that extended all the way from the Atlantic Ocean to the Pacific. The country would be well settled from coast to coast. The "western wilderness" would be tamed and transformed into productive land, prosperous settlements, and centers of trade. In order to make this dream a reality, the United States would have to acquire the Louisiana Territory from Spain and explore and establish possession of its vast lands. Jefferson was so focused on this goal that he collected many books on the Louisiana Territory, establishing a library that included more volumes on this topic than any other collection in the world.

The Treaty of San Ildefonso

Shortly after Jefferson became president in March 1801, a threat to Jefferson's vision of an expanded United States emerged. Disturbing rumors began circulating of a secret agreement between France and Spain. The stories claimed that Spain had given the territories of Louisiana, New Orleans, and East and West Florida to France. In 1801 there were two Floridas: West Florida and East Florida. East Florida included most of the present-day state of Florida. West Florida included what would become the southern portions of Alabama and Mississippi, and a portion of Louisiana.

At the turn of the nineteenth century, Spain was declining as a world power. It posed little threat to America and its interests. President Jefferson was far more concerned by France and its intentions. A powerful and dynamic country, France was led by the ambitious and aggressive dictator Napoléon Bonaparte. Napoléon was a military genius who had already conquered much of Europe. With Spain's decline, Napoléon saw an opportunity to extend his vast empire into North America as well. The Louisiana Territory, with New Orleans as the political and economic center, would be

Napoléon's foothold in the New World, from which he could continue to conquer more and more lands. Napoléon's dream of conquest would present a serious obstacle to Jefferson's own ambitions for the United States's expansion.

Robert Livingston, the American minister to France, tried to determine whether the rumors of a land transfer were true, but French officials ignored his questions. Finally in 1802, the United States discovered that the stories concerning Spain's transfer of the Louisiana Territory to France were indeed accurate. The two countries had already signed a secret treaty, the Treaty of San Ildefonso, on October 1, 1800. In this document, Spain had agreed to give the Louisiana Territory to France in return for

Tuscany, a valuable region of Italy. It remained unclear exactly how much North American land was involved in the transfer. The treaty stated only that Spain ceded to France the province of Louisiana as it was when France had first owned it, with no changes to the territory's borders. At the very least, the treaty gave France control of New Orleans and all the land west of the Mississippi River to the Rocky Mountains. It was not clear, however, whether the important Spanish territories of East and West Florida, which bordered the Gulf of Mexico, were also included in the deal.

The Importance of New Orleans

The port at New Orleans was a particularly valuable asset and of special importance to the United States. Since there were still no roads that connected the western territories of the United States to the cities and markets on the East Coast, Americans sent their goods to market via the Mississippi River. Farmers from places like Illinois and Kentucky sent their crops down the river to New Orleans, then into the Gulf of Mexico, around Florida, and up the East Coast. Fur traders in the western wilderness also had to transport their goods to New Orleans using the Mississippi River. From there, the goods were shipped either to the East Coast or to Europe. By the early 1800s, the Mississippi had become a major highway for trade and commerce, with New Orleans a crucial port on this great waterway.

In years past, Spain had offered United States citizens free access to the Mississippi River and the "right of deposit" at New Orleans. This meant that Americans could ship their goods down the river and through New Orleans without having to pay any duties or taxes to Spanish authorities. A tax upon shipping at

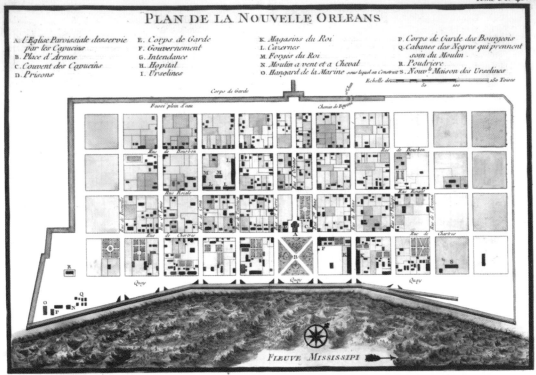

This is a 1764 plan of New Orleans created by the French mapmaker Jacques Nicolas Bellin. With the Mississippi River running along the bottom, the city streets, blocks, and buildings are viewed as if from above. The location of important public buildings, such as churches, hospitals, prisons, armories, and barracks, are indicated and listed along the top.

New Orleans would increase the expenses of the farmers, trappers, and merchants, seriously crippling American trade.

President Jefferson was very worried that, after taking formal possession of New Orleans, the French would institute such a tax. In order to protect American trade, he instructed his representative Robert Livingston to travel to Paris and try to buy New Orleans and East and West Florida from the French. If the French would not agree to sell those lands, at the very least the United States wanted a guarantee of free passage down the Mississippi River and trading rights at the port of New Orleans.

For weeks, Livingston tried to persuade the French to sell New Orleans and the Floridas to the United States, but his efforts were unsuccessful. After many attempts at negotiation, Livingston became very frustrated with his lack of progress.

On October 15, 1802, Jefferson's worst fears were realized. The French took away from the United States the right of free access at New Orleans. Americans could still use the Mississippi River and trade their goods in New Orleans, but from now on they would have to pay duties and port fees, just like any other foreign trader.

Western Americans were shocked and outraged. They felt that free access to the Mississippi River and New Orleans was something to which they were entitled. In their minds, being charged taxes was the same as being denied use of the river and the port. They protested loudly and demanded that President Jefferson and Congress do something to protect their interests.

The anger of the western settlers was so intense that Jefferson became concerned that they might even consider seceding from the United States. If the United States did not act immediately, the frontiersmen might take matters into their own hands. There was wild talk of taking up arms and launching an expedition down the Mississippi to capture New Orleans. Jefferson was determined to obtain the vital trading port of New Orleans for the United States, in part to prevent its western territories from breaking away.

Even Americans on the East Coast were concerned about events in New Orleans because they needed the goods that the westerners shipped through that port city. Any interruption to deliveries would cut into the merchants' profits, as would any tax imposed upon those goods. The extra costs would be passed on to the consumer, making it harder for families to make ends meet. Something had to be done to insure free access to the port of New Orleans.

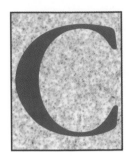

CHAPTER 3

In January 1803, Jefferson decided to send James Monroe to Paris to assist Robert Livingston in the negotiations with the French. Monroe was a former governor of Virginia and a former minister to France. He was also known to be a friend of the western Americans. Jefferson hoped that his appointment would reassure the frontier settlers that their interests would be guarded carefully. On March 8, 1803, James Monroe sailed for France, arriving in Paris on April 12.

Upon arrival, Robert Livingston quickly informed Monroe that negotiations with the French had so far proved unsuccessful. He told Monroe that, in his opinion, the only way that the United States would gain free access to New Orleans would be by force.

A SURPRISING OFFER

The following evening, while Monroe and Livingston were eating dinner, they received a surprise visit from François Barbé-Marbois, the French minister of the treasury. Livingston and Monroe were astonished when the French official informed them that, after refusing their far smaller request for access to New Orleans, Napoléon was suddenly interested in selling the entire Louisiana Territory to the United States. The two Americans knew it was an opportunity that would never come their way again and that they could not pass it up.

Before becoming the ambassador to France, Robert R. Livingston *(top left)* was a member of the five-man committee responsible for drafting the Declaration of Independence. He also administered the presidential oath of office to George Washington in 1789. James Monroe *(bottom right)* served in the American Revolution and was minister to France from 1794 to 1796. He would become the fifth president of the United States in 1816.

Napoléon's Reasons

There were a number of reasons why Napoléon decided to offer the sale of the Louisiana Territory to the United States. The primary one was that he needed to raise enough money to wage a war that was brewing with Great Britain.

In addition, Napoléon had once hoped to create a French stronghold in the Americas, with Hispaniola as its capital. (Hispaniola is an island of the West Indies divided between Haiti and the Dominican Republic.) Yet, in 1802, he lost control of the island to a successful revolt of the island's slaves. As a result, Louisiana no longer seemed necessary to him. He felt he might as well sell his North American interests because he believed that the United States or England might try to seize those colonies while he was absorbed in fighting a difficult war in Europe. He had heard about the rumors of fifty thousand American frontiersmen ready and able to take New Orleans by force. United States newspapers talked of reports of the war fever that was spreading among America's western settlers. Napoléon would never be able to defend such a vast territory, especially if he was simultaneously waging war in Europe. Why not sell the now useless territory before it was stolen from him?

Another reason that Napoléon offered the Louisiana Territory to America was simply because France and the United States shared a common enemy—Great Britain. Selling the Louisiana Territory to the United States prevented the land from falling into English hands and strengthened the position of a fellow enemy of the empire. Most important, Great Britain would not gain any greater influence in the New World, which could have shifted the balance of power in Europe in England's favor.

Problems Arise

While France's offer to sell the entire Louisiana Territory to the United States appeared to be good news, Livingston and Monroe were worried that if they accepted the deal, they would be going beyond the objectives Jefferson had assigned them. After all, they were supposed to negotiate the ownership of New Orleans and East and West Florida. They were not authorized to purchase the entire Louisiana Territory.

Unsure of how to proceed, Livingston and Monroe considered sending a message to Jefferson to inform him of Napoléon's surprising offer. But because the only way to send messages from Europe to America back then was by ship, it could take several weeks to send a message to Jefferson and then to receive his reply. Even though Napoléon made it clear that he needed the funds from the sale to finance his war with Great Britain, he also let it be known that he would cancel the offer if the Americans did not act immediately and decisively.

A further source of confusion was the actual land involved in the deal. Livingston and Monroe did not know the exact boundaries of the territory they were being offered. It was generally agreed that the Louisiana Territory extended west from the Mississippi River to the Rocky Mountains and from the Gulf of Mexico in the south to the Canadian border in the north. But Livingston and Monroe were not sure if East or West Florida was also included in the agreement, and the French did not offer a clear answer. In addition, the French failed to inform the Americans that Napoléon had promised the Spanish king that he would not cede Louisiana to any country other than Spain.

In spite of this confusion and uncertainty, the Americans decided to go ahead with the purchase, but not without qualms

The PRAIRIE DOG sickened at the sting of the HORNET — or a Diplomatic Puppet exhibiting his Deceptions!

Though it is now viewed as the greatest real estate deal in history, Jefferson's purchase of Louisiana had many critics. This circa 1804 political cartoon by James Akin shows President Thomas Jefferson in the form of a prairie dog vomiting up the money paid to France for the new territory. To his rear, Napoléon, in the form of a hornet, stings him, while a French diplomat dances before him saying, "A gull [fool] for the people." This cartoon reflected a widespread opinion that Jefferson foolishly spent millions of taxpayers' dollars on worthless land.

about money. When Monroe and Livingston were first sent to try to purchase New Orleans, Congress voted to pay as much as $2 million for the port city, but Jefferson privately authorized the two men to go up to $10 million, if necessary. Now, however, the French were asking for more than $17 million. Granted, Monroe and Livingston were being offered all of Louisiana, but they were also being asked to spend $7 million more than they were allowed for unexplored territory that many people considered a vast wasteland. So, for several days, the Americans bargained with the French over the price of the Louisiana Purchase. In the end, Napoléon agreed to $15 million in exchange for more than 820,000 square miles (2.1 million sq km) of land—about three cents an acre. Quite a bargain, especially by today's standards!

Before the Louisiana Purchase could be made official, both President Jefferson and Congress had to approve the agreement. Amazed and elated by the offer, Jefferson accepted and rushed the treaty through Congress, in spite of doubts about its constitutionality. Some people felt that the Constitution did not give the president the power to spend public money on new territory without first consulting Congress and the individual states. Political enemies attacked the purchase not only as an unconstitutional use of executive power, but also as a waste of money. They felt that the land was a useless, uninhabitable wilderness and could not imagine a day when the present borders of the United States could not comfortably contain all the nation's citizens. They could not foresee that the country would prosper to such an extent that it would continuously expand westward and eventually settle the frontier from the Mississippi River to the Pacific Ocean.

Jefferson knew that the Constitution did not spell out whether the national government could buy foreign lands. The Constitution did, however, provide for the making of treaties with other countries. Jefferson reasoned that the deal could be considered a treaty with France as much as a land purchase. Seen in this light, it did not violate the spirit of the Constitution. Though convinced he was acting in the best interests of his young country and providing for its future growth and prosperity, Jefferson recognized that he had probably "stretched things" to convince Congress and the public of the legality of the purchase.

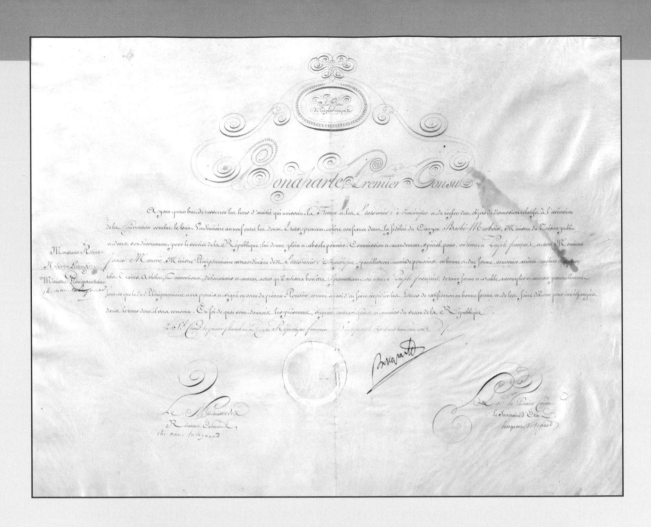

In any event, the majority of the House of Representatives and Senate, as well as much of the American public, was overwhelmingly in favor of purchasing Louisiana. The United States Senate ratified the treaty on October 20, 1803, by a vote of twenty-seven to seven. The same day, the House of Representatives authorized borrowing money from European banks to pay for the Louisiana Territory.

A Peaceful Transfer

The Spanish were furious when they learned of the sale. They complained that the United States had no right to Louisiana because France had promised never to transfer the territory to any other country. The Americans replied that this was not their concern. Fortunately for the Americans, there was little Spain could do against the combined strength and determination of France and the United States.

Confronted with a done deal and left with few options, Spain attempted to preserve some pride and strategic advantage by insisting that the Louisiana Purchase did not include the Floridas. The United States tried to claim West Florida as part of the deal, but its claim was denied. Finally, on November 30, 1803, in a ceremony in New Orleans, Spain stopped protesting and formally transferred the Louisiana Territory to France. (Spain had never given up physical possession of Louisiana to

At top is Napoléon's authorization for the sale by France of the Louisiana Territory to the United States. His bold, underlined signature appears in the center bottom. In the print below it, Napoléon is shown discussing the Louisiana Purchase Treaty with his ministers Charles Maurice de Talleyrand-Périgord and François Barbé-Marbois. The 1904 print, by H. Davidson, is based upon an original image by Andre Castaigne.

Treaty

Between the United States of America
and the French Republic

The President of the United States of America and the First
Consul of the French Republic in the name of the French
People desiring to remove all Source of misunderstanding ————
relative to objects of discussion mentioned in the Second
and fifth articles of the Convention of the {8th Vendemiaire an 9 / 30 September 1800}
relative to the rights claimed by the United States in virtue of
the Treaty concluded at Madrid the 27 of October 1795, between
His Catholic Majesty, & the Said United States, & willing to
Strengthen the union and friendship which at the time of
the Said Convention was happily reestablished between the two
nations have respectively named their Plenipotentiaries to wit
The President of the United States, by and with the advice
and consent of the Senate of the Said States; Robert R.
Livingston Minister Plenipotentiary
and James Monroe Minister Pleni-
extraordinary of the Said State near the
French Republic; And the First C
of the French people, Citizen Franc
Minister of the public treasury who
vely exchanged their full powers have

the French. Twenty days later, the United States received Louisiana from France.

The American flag was raised over New Orleans for the first time on December 20, 1803, after a formal transfer document was signed. With a single stroke of the pen, the size of the United States was doubled! According to the office of the secretary of state of Louisiana, Robert Livingston declared of the peaceful transfer, "We have lived long, but this is the noblest work of our whole lives . . . From this day, the United States will take their place among the powers of the first rank . . . The instruments which we have just signed will cause no tears to be shed; they prepare ages of happiness for innumerable generations of human creatures."

The Louisiana Purchase Treaty, signed in Paris on April 30, 1803, is actually a three-part document. The first part concerns the territory in question and its transfer to the United States. The second part details the sum of money the United States is to pay for the territory. The final section is an agreement by the United States to pay the sums of money owed by the French government to U.S. citizens in Louisiana (amounting to $3,750,000). At top left is the first page of the treaty. The inset shows the bound copy of the treaty housed in the National Archives. For a partial transcript of the treaty, see pages 54–56.

CHAPTER 4

LEWIS AND CLARK'S CORPS OF DISCOVERY

On December 21, 1803, Americans woke up in a country that was twice as big as it had been the day before. While the Louisiana Purchase had greatly increased the size of the United States, the borders of the new territory were still unclear, and the land itself was mysterious and unexplored. Many considered it to be an uninhabitable wasteland. No one knew exactly how large the new territory was or who or what it contained. For Jefferson's dream of westward expansion and settlement to become a reality, merely owning the land west of the Mississippi River would not be enough. It would have to be explored, occupied, and effectively defended.

Fulfilling Jefferson's Vision

Even before the Louisiana Purchase was completed and the territory officially handed over to the United States, Jefferson had begun making plans for a "Corps of Discovery." This group of adventurers would establish an official American presence in the territory, explore the new lands, and begin to forge diplomatic and trade relations with the western Native American nations. On January 18, 1803, Jefferson sent Congress a secret message requesting the $2,500 he would need to fund the expedition to

William Clark *(top left)* and Meriwether Lewis *(bottom right)* are pictured here in 1807 portraits painted by Charles Willson Peale. Both men were born into Virginia plantation families that included members who were Revolutionary War veterans. Both men joined militias as young men and went on to serve as officers in the U.S. Army. They first met in Fort Greenville, Ohio, where Clark briefly served as Lewis's commanding officer. Several years later, Lewis would "rescue" Clark from a sedate farmer's life he did not want by inviting him to co-captain the Corps of Discovery's adventurous expedition.

37

the West. (Actual costs would reach $38,722 by the time the expedition came to an end.)

Following congressional approval of Jefferson's plan to explore the newly purchased Louisiana Territory in February of 1803, Jefferson appointed his secretary, Meriwether Lewis, a political ally and fellow Virginian, to lead the expedition. Lewis was allowed to personally select his second in command. He chose an old army friend, William Clark, with whom he had served in the Northwest Territory. Although Clark was not as educated as Lewis, he was cheerful, a keen observer, a conscientious journal writer, and a skilled cartographer (mapmaker). Lewis was shy, liked science and nature, was experienced in wilderness life, and was also a talented cartographer. Though they differed in basic personality, the moody Lewis and more even-tempered Clark made a compatible, strong team.

The Corps of Discovery's Goals

What did Jefferson want the Lewis and Clark expedition to achieve? The president was keenly interested in learning more about the natural features of the western lands. He sent Lewis off with several pages of specific instructions about what information to collect during the journey. Both Lewis and Clark were asked to keep their own journals in which to record everything they observed and experienced. Most of the other expedition members kept journals as well. In addition, Lewis and Clark were instructed to draw maps, record scientific observations, and collect specimens of western plants, animals, and minerals.

Jefferson also wanted Lewis and Clark to observe and make contact with the western Indians. He wanted the corps to study their customs, languages, and medical practices, while also learning from

of small fish which now begin to run and are taken in great quantities in the Columbia R. about 40 miles above us by means of skiming or scooping nets. on this page I have drawn the likeness of them as large as life; it as perfect as I can make it with my pen and will serve to give a general idea of the fish. the rays of the fins are boney but not sharp tho' somewhat pointed. the small fin on the back next to the tail has no rays of bone being a membraneous pellicle. to the gills have each. those of the eight each, those are 20 and 2 that of the back the fins are of is of a bleuish the the lower is of a silve= part. the behid the second of the purple a silver and like

93

Salmon Trout No. 61.

thin mem the fins next eleven rays abdomen have of the pinnate half formed in front. has eleven rays. all a white colour. the back dusky colour and that of part of the sides and belly a white. no spots on any first bone of the gills next eye is of a bluis cast, and the a light gold colour nearly white of the eye is black and the iris of white. the under jaw exceeds the uper; the mouth opens to great extent, folding; that of the herring. it has no teeth. the abdomen is obtuse and smooth; in this differing from the herring, shad anchovy; &c of the Malacapterygious Order & Class Clupea

Because of his keen interest in science, President Thomas Jefferson requested that all members of the corps keep detailed journals to record their impressions and observations of the previously unexplored western lands. Lewis's knowledge of botany (the study of plants) and zoology (the study of animals) resulted in some valuable and fascinating notes. Above is a page from Lewis's journal, dated February 24, 1806, in which he has sketched a life-size eulachon, or candlefish, accompanied by his descriptions and observations. In the course of the expedition, the Corps of Discovery recorded 178 plants and 122 animals not previously known to exist. See transcript on page 56.

the Native Americans about the natural features of the recently acquired land. While the Louisiana Territory was a new acquisition for the United States, it had been home to Native Americans for thousands of years, and they were intimately familiar with the terrain. Jefferson hoped to form alliances with the various Indian tribes that would promote security and peace in the frontier and also encourage trade. The United States wanted to edge out France and England and become the main seller of goods to the Indian nations. In exchange for products like tobacco, alcohol, guns, and ammunition, American traders would receive animal pelts from the Native Americans, thereby gaining control of the lucrative fur trade.

Indeed, one of the primary goals of the expedition was to create new possibilities for trade. Jefferson hoped that Lewis and Clark would find the fabled Northwest Passage—a water route running between the Atlantic and Pacific coasts that could provide a more direct link between Europe and North America and markets in Asia. If such a passage existed, it would also allow western goods to be shipped back east far more quickly than over the existing land and river routes.

During the spring and summer of 1803, correspondence passed back and forth between Thomas Jefferson, Captain Meriwether Lewis, and Captain William Clark about plans for the trip and qualifications of the men needed for the expedition. All of the men were handpicked—the two captains for their leadership qualities and the rest for hunting, woodcutting, frontier, craftsmanship, interpreting, navigating, and other desirable skills.

The Travels of Lewis and Clark

Lewis left Philadelphia in the summer of 1803 and joined Clark and a few recruits in Indiana before arriving late in the year at the

This contemporary painting by Ed Fisher, entitled *Lewis and Clark at St. Charles, May 21, 1804*, depicts the departure of the Corps of Discovery from the banks of the Missouri River in St. Charles, Missouri. The keelboat and two canoe-like pirogues can be seen setting out on what would turn out to be a two-and-a-half-year journey of discovery. The keelboat could be rowed by twenty men or towed with the help of ropes by men walking along the riverbank. It also had a sail, but this was rarely used.

staging area near St. Louis. There they met their team of explorers, who gathered on the eastern bank of the Missouri River.

They loaded the supplies onto their three boats. The largest was a keelboat, fifty-five feet long with a square sail and twenty-two oars for rowing. The other two boats were large dugout canoes known as pirogues. One canoe had six oars, the other had seven. The supplies included clothing, tools, blankets, knapsacks, tools, guns, food, and medical equipment. The corps also brought things to trade with the Native Americans—beads, ribbons, American flags, fishhooks, and needles. Also on hand were peace and friendship medals that Lewis and Clark presented to Native American chiefs to encourage friendship and harmony with the new American rulers of the land.

After making their final preparations, Lewis and Clark set off on May 14, 1804, ascending the Mississippi River to the mouth of the Missouri River and then westward. Over the next two and a half years, the Corps of Discovery would repeatedly put their strength, endurance, and skills to the test, paddling and sailing up the Missouri, crossing endless barren wastes and cruel jagged mountains, and surviving hunger, fierce cold, and a small number of hostile Native American tribes.

Discovering and Documenting the New Land

As the explorers crossed the Great Plains, they saw a wide variety of plants and animals that had never been observed and recorded by Europeans. From North Dakota all the way to the West Coast, Lewis and Clark passed through lands that no Europeans had ever seen before. In November 1805, they reached their goal—the Pacific Ocean.

Lewis and Clark brought back hundreds of scientific specimens. In fact, they are credited with discovering approximately 178 plants and 122 animals that were unknown to North American science at the time. Many of the plant and animal specimens, artifacts, maps, and written and sketched observations were sent back to President Jefferson. Live animals, journals, and other items journeyed down the Missouri and the Mississippi to New Orleans, then went by sailing ship to Baltimore, finally arriving in Washington four months later. One magpie and a prairie dog reached Jefferson alive. The prairie dog lived for several months after its arrival at the Peale Museum in Philadelphia.

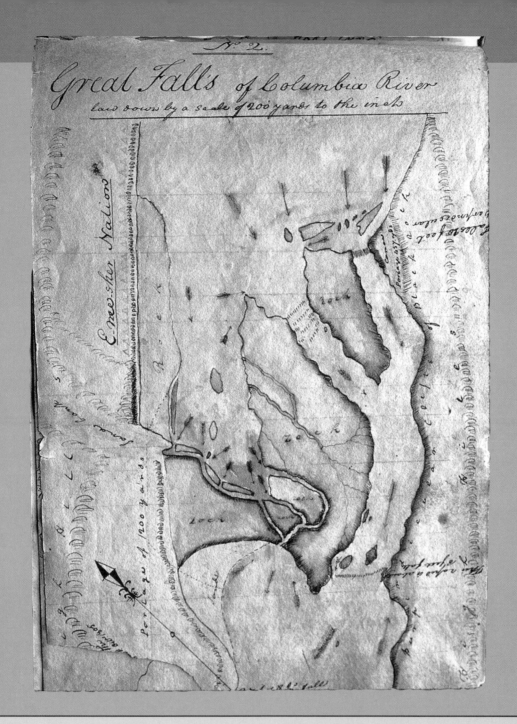

Great Falls of Columbia River
laid down by a scale of 200 yards to the inch

This is a sketch by William Clark of the Great Falls of the Columbia River made in October 1805. When the Corps of Discovery arrived at the banks of the Columbia in the fall, the river was full of salmon that were completing their annual spawning migration upriver. They entered what is now the state of Washington in October 1805, reaching the Pacific on November 6. After spending a few days exploring the area around the mouth of the Columbia River, they began construction of their winter quarters in December, naming it Fort Clatsop after the local Clatsop tribe. The winter that the corps spent at Fort Clatsop was a miserable one—wet, dreary, and short on food.

At the completion of their journey, Lewis and Clark returned with a large archive of maps that pinpointed towering mountains, raging rivers, and rustic forests and with extensive, detailed notes on the climate, soil, plants, and animals of the West. All of this information greatly expanded Americans' understanding and knowledge of the western frontier, eventually making trade and settlement west of the Mississippi a far more attractive and realistic option. Just two years after the Louisiana Purchase, the Wild West was already beginning to be tamed.

Sacagawea

Perhaps the best-known person to take part in the Corps of Discovery, other than Lewis and Clark themselves, was not a man but a Native American woman named Sacagawea. Sacagawea's role in the Lewis and Clark expedition is widely recognized, yet we know very little about her. In fact, historians are not even sure about her name. Meriwether Lewis recorded her name as "Sah-ca-gar-me-ah." Modern writers have used both "Sacajawea" and "Sakakawea" in addition to the now preferred "Sacagawea." Her name might have been a Hidatsa word for "bird woman" or a Shoshone word meaning "boat launcher." (Sacagawea was a Shoshone Indian who was later kidnapped by a Hidatsa tribe.)

Sacagawea was born around 1788 among the Lemhi Shoshone in what is now western Montana or Idaho. At about twelve years old, she was captured by a Hidatsa raiding party and taken to North Dakota. A French Canadian fur trader named Toussaint Charbonneau bought or won her in 1804 while she was living with the Hidatsa and made her one of his two wives. She gave birth to her first child, a boy named Jean Baptiste, early the next year.

When Lewis and Clark reached North Dakota in the winter of 1804, they met Sacagawea and Charbonneau and hired them both as interpreters. Sacagawea was very helpful in dealing with the many Native American tribes the corps encountered and was instrumental in helping the explorers obtain horses from them. Since she was a Native American, other Native Americans seemed to relax when they noticed her among the group of white explorers. This helped Lewis and Clark establish a friendly relationship with many of the tribes they met. Needless to say, this proved to be extremely helpful to the expedition because the various tribes were able to help them by describing the upcoming terrain and possible dangers, locating landmarks (like waterfalls), telling them which animals and plants were edible, and occasionally providing them with food and horses.

For almost two years, Sacagawea traveled with the corps while carrying and caring for her young son, providing help for the expedition, and risking her life every day to do so. At one point, she became seriously ill, but luckily, with Lewis and Clark's medical help, she recovered. Had she died, her four-month-old baby would have been left without a mother. Lewis and Clark would have lost their only Shoshone interpreter and mediator, an important guide, and a respected member of the expedition.

Native Americans

While Lewis and Clark were the first Americans to see much of what would become the western United States, that territory had long been the home of many tribes of native people. Over the course of the expedition, the Corps of Discovery would come into contact with more than forty Native American tribes. Lewis and Clark were amazed by the widely varying attitudes

At top is an engraving depicting a Mandan village. At the center of the picture is a cedar post surrounded by a plank fence. This is a replica of the Sacred Ark. Like Jews and Christians, the Mandan had a flood myth. The First Man (equivalent to Adam) saved his people by teaching them how to build an ark or protective tower that would save them from the rising floodwaters. The poles wrapped with feathers represent an evil spirit who has power over humans but is weaker than the First Man. The inset depicts a Mandan man.

and lifestyles of the various Native American nations. For example, the Mandans lived in earth lodges, farmed corn, and were open to trade with Americans. The Teton Sioux, on the other hand, slept in tepees, hunted buffalo, and guarded their territory fiercely against anyone who passed through, whether foreign or Native American. Some tribes had never seen a white or black man before the arrival of the Corps of Discovery.

When meeting a tribe for the first time, Lewis and Clark would explain to the tribal leaders that their land now belonged to the United States, and that a man in the East—President Jefferson—was their new "Great Father." They would also give the Native Americans a peace medal with Jefferson on one side and two clasped hands on the other, as well as some form of present. Corps members would usually perform a kind of parade, marching in uniform and shooting their guns into the air.

Unlike many who followed, the explorers were generally cooperative with the native peoples they met and were grateful for their help and cooperation. Very few of their encounters with Native American tribes resulted in hostility or violence. The two captains were able to establish a peaceful relationship with many of the approximately forty tribes with which they made contact. In addition, they described the customs, languages, and artifacts of many of these eastern and western tribes in their journals in detail.

Homeward Bound

Using all of their physical and emotional strength and resources, Lewis and Clark overcame enormous hardships with imagination and a positive attitude, and they carried out every one of President Jefferson's goals for the expedition, reaching the

Pacific Ocean in late November 1805. Thanks to the corps' extraordinary efforts, future explorers and settlers were armed with accurate information about the land, the animals, the weather, and the people of the vast western lands newly acquired by the United States. Jefferson's trust in Lewis and Clark proved to be well placed.

The corps's return journey began on March 23, 1806. On Sunday, September 21, 1806, they finally emerged out of the wilderness. Arriving in the village of St. Charles (near St. Louis), the jubilant explorers were greeted by surprised and cheering crowds. They had been gone for more than two years and four months. Upon returning, the men discovered that they had been given up for dead long ago.

A Journey into History

Meriwether Lewis and William Clark were the two brave, adventurous men whom President Thomas Jefferson trusted enough to send out to explore America's precious and mysterious new land. In a daring expedition, joined by thirty to forty other explorers, they walked, paddled, and rode horses from St. Louis (then a frontier outpost) to the Pacific Ocean. Their history-making journey covered more than 8,000 miles (12,875 km) of previously unexplored territory.

Above is a map of the American West first begun by William Clark at Fort Clatsop, the stockade the corps built near present-day Astoria, Oregon, in December 1805. He worked on the map throughout the wet, dreary winter of 1805–1806. Once completed, this map provided the most detailed depiction of the rivers, plains, mountains, and lakes west of the Mississippi ever recorded. Below it is a map that shows the route taken by the Corps of Discovery.

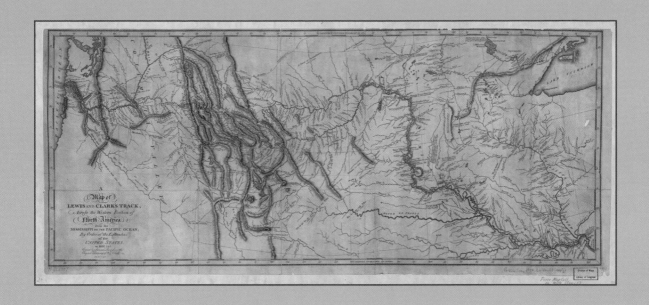

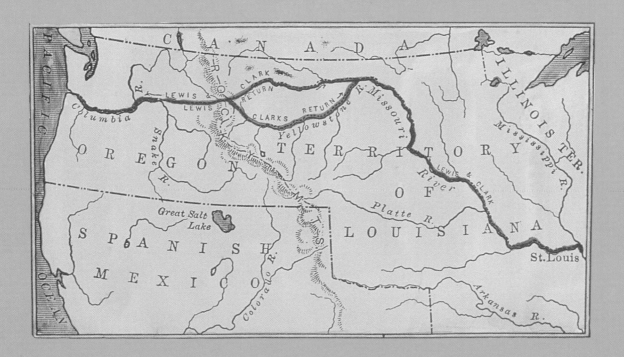

In the time it took to place a signature on a document, the Louisiana Purchase moved the nation's western boundary from the Mississippi River to the Rocky Mountains. Lewis and Clark's two-and-a-half-year expedition made the newly acquired land—previously the province of myth and folk legend—a concrete reality for Americans. Lewis and Clark helped to establish American control of its vast new territory, forge initially friendly relations with many of the western Native American nations, trace new trade routes, map the wilderness, and make important scientific discoveries about the land, plants, and animals of the territory. Most important, the Corps of Discovery made possible the eventual settlement of the western lands acquired through the Louisiana Purchase, creating a nation that would span the entire continent.

CHAPTER 5

A DREAM COME TRUE

Following the Louisiana Purchase and the Lewis and Clark expedition, settlers from the East were gradually drawn westward, lured by the promise of cheap and open land, new opportunities to make money, and greater personal freedom. With westward expansion and the growth of settlements and trade, the previously vast and unbounded land began to be organized into governable units.

In 1804, the Louisiana Territory was divided into two separate territories—the District of Louisiana (which later became the Missouri Territory) lay north of the 33rd parallel, while the Territory of Orleans lay south of it. Both territories stretched from the Mississippi River to the east and the Rockies to the west. In 1812, the Territory of Orleans and a small part of West Florida entered the union as the eighteenth state— Louisiana. West Florida had been seized by American citizens in 1810 but was still claimed by Spain and not formally ceded to the United States until 1821. By 1889, thirteen states had been carved out of the original Louisiana Purchase: Louisiana, Arkansas, Oklahoma, Missouri, Kansas, Nebraska, Iowa, South Dakota, North Dakota, Wyoming, Minnesota, Colorado, and Montana.

The Louisiana Purchase is one of the most unique territorial expansions in history in that it was acquired without bloodshed

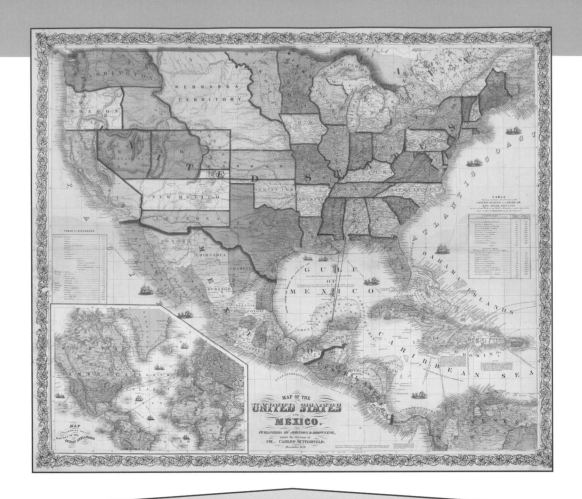

This is a map created by the mapmakers Johnson & Browning that shows all of the states and territories of the United States as of 1859, including those that were eventually carved out of the Louisiana Purchase of 1803. The map offers graphic evidence of the new settlement and trade opportunities made possible by Lewis and Clark's exploration of the country's western lands. Their courageous journey of exploration gave many Americans the knowledge they needed to take their chances and venture west of the Mississippi River to begin new lives, businesses, and communities on the American frontier.

(though its eventual settlement would result in the death and displacement of millions of Native Americans). It gave the United States valuable new land, doubled the young country's size, introduced new cultures and citizens into the union, and eventually allowed the country's borders to expand west of the Rocky Mountains all the way to the Pacific Ocean. "The acquisition is great and glorious in itself but still greater and more glorious are the means by which it is obtained," proclaimed a leading newspaper, the *National Intelligencer*, in January 1804. Never in history, the newspaper boasted, had so much land been exchanged so peacefully. Or so cheaply. As General Horatio Gates wrote to President Thomas Jefferson on July 18, 1803, "Let the Land rejoice, for you have bought Louisiana for a Song" (as quoted on the National Archives and Records Administration Web site.)

Above all, the Louisiana Purchase opened the way for westward expansion and the realization of Thomas Jefferson's vision of a great nation that stretched from the Atlantic to the Pacific. According to the National Louisiana Purchase Bicentennial Committee, in 1904, just more than a century after the Louisiana Territory was acquired by the United States, President Theodore Roosevelt declared that the purchase was "the event which more than any other, after the foundation of the Government ... determined the character of our national life." The United States of the twenty-first century—its land, its towns and cities, its wealth, its diversity, its industrious frontier spirit—is largely a legacy of the Louisiana Purchase. Thomas Jefferson's vision of a large, prosperous, secure, and free nation has been realized. America has become what he always dreamed it could be.

PRIMARY SOURCE TRANSCRIPTIONS

Page 34: The Louisiana Purchase Treaty, Signed on April 30, 1803, in Paris, France by Robert Livingston, James Monroe, and François Barbé-Marbois

Excerpted Transcription

Treaty Between the United States of America and the French Republic

The President of the United States of America [Thomas Jefferson] and the First Consul of the French Republic [Napoléon Bonaparte] in the name of the French People desiring to remove all Source of misunderstanding relative to objects of discussion mentioned in the Second and fifth articles of the Convention of the 8th Vendé miaire [the first month of the French revolutionary calendar] on 9/30 September 1800 [the Treaty of San Ildefonso] relative to the rights claimed by the United States in virtue of the Treaty concluded at Madrid the 27 of October 1795, between His Catholic Majesty [King Charles IV of Spain] & the Said United States [a peace treaty that established the boundaries between Spanish and U.S. territories and granted the U.S. free access to the Mississippi River and the port of New Orleans], & willing to Strengthen the union and friendship which at the time of the Said Convention was happily reestablished between the two nations have respectively named their Plenipotentiaries to wit The President of the United States, by and with the advice and consent of the Senate of the Said States; Robert R. Livingston Minister Plenipotentiary of the United States and James Monroe Minister Plenipotentiary and Envoy extraordinary of the Said States near the Government of the French Republic; And the First Consul in the name of the French people, Citizen Francis Barbé Marbois Minister of the public treasury who after having respectively exchanged their full powers have agreed to the following Articles.

Article I [stating that Spain agrees to transfer the Louisiana Territory to France so that France can transfer it to the United States]

Whereas by the Article the third of the Treaty concluded at St Ildefonso the 9th Vendé miaire an 9/1st October 1800 between the First Consul of the French Republic and his Catholic Majesty it was agreed as follows.

"His Catholic Majesty promises and engages on his part to cede to the French Republic six months after the full and entire execution of the conditions and Stipulations herein relative to his Royal Highness the Duke of Parma, the Colony or Province of Louisiana with the Same extent that it now has in the hand of Spain, & that it had when France possessed it; and Such as it Should be after the Treaties subsequently entered into between Spain and other States."

And whereas in pursuance of the Treaty and particularly of the third article the French Republic has an incontestible title to the domain and to the possession of the said Territory—The First Consul of the French Republic desiring to give to the United States a strong proof of his friendship doth hereby cede to the United States in the name of the French Republic for ever and in full Sovereignty the said territory with all its rights and appurtenances as fully and in the Same manner as they have been acquired by the French Republic in virtue of the above mentioned Treaty concluded with his Catholic Majesty.

Art: II [transferring all land, buildings, and other public property in the Louisiana Territory to the United States]

In the cession made by the preceeding article are included the adjacent Islands belonging to Louisiana all public lots and Squares, vacant lands and all public buildings, fortifications, barracks and other edifices which are not private property.—The Archives, papers & documents relative to the domain and Sovereignty of Louisiana and its dependances will be left in the possession of the Commissaries of the United States, and copies will be afterwards given in due form to the Magistrates and Municipal officers of such of the said papers and documents as may be necessary to them.

Art: III [the incorporation of Louisiana residents into the United States]

The inhabitants of the ceded territory shall be incorporated in the Union of the United States and admitted as soon as possible according to the principles of the federal Constitution to the enjoyment of all these rights, advantages and immunities of citizens of the United States, and in the mean time they shall be maintained and protected in the free enjoyment of their liberty, property and the Religion which they profess...

Art: V [the departure of the French and Spanish militaries from Louisiana]

Immediately after the ratification of the present Treaty by the President of the United States and in case that of the first Consul's shall have been previously obtained, the commissary of the French Republic shall remit all military posts of New Orleans and other parts of the ceded territory to the Commissary or Commissaries named by the President to take possession—the troops whether of France or Spain who may be there shall cease to occupy any military post from the time of taking possession and shall be embarked as soon as possible in the course of three months after the ratification of this treaty.

Art: VI [the United States's commitment to honoring Spanish treaties with Indian nations]

The United States promise to execute Such treaties and articles as may have been agreed between Spain and the tribes and nations of Indians until by mutual consent of the United States and the said tribes or nations other Suitable articles Shall have been agreed upon.

Art: VII [insuring the rights of France and Spain to have continued free access to the Mississippi River and the port of New Orleans for a period of twelve years]

As it is reciprocally advantageous to the commerce of France and the United States to encourage the communication of both nations for a limited time in the country ceded by the present treaty until general arrangements relative to commerce of both nations may be agreed on; it has been agreed between the contracting parties that the French Ships coming directly from France or any of her colonies loaded only with the produce and manufactures of France or her Said Colonies; and the Ships of Spain coming directly from Spain or any of her colonies loaded only with the produce or manufactures of Spain or her Colonies shall be admitted during the Space of twelve years in the Port of New-Orleans and in all other legal ports-of-entry within the ceded territory in the Same manner as the Ships of the United States coming directly from France or Spain or any of their Colonies without being Subject to any other or greater duty on merchandize or other or greater tonnage than that paid by the citizens of the United. States.

During that Space of time above mentioned no other nation Shall have a right to the Same privileges in the Ports of the ceded territory—the twelve years Shall commence three months after the exchange of ratifications if it Shall take place in France or three months after it Shall have been notified at Paris to the French Government if it Shall take place in the United States; It is however well understood that the object of the above article is to favour the manufactures, Commerce, freight and navigation of France and of Spain So far as relates to the importations that the French and Spanish Shall make into the Said Ports of the United States without in any Sort affecting the regulations that the United States may make concerning the exportation of the produce and merchandize of the United States, or any right they may have to make Such regulations…

Art: X [timetable for ratification of treaty]

The present treaty Shall be ratified in good and due form and the ratifications Shall be exchanged in the Space of Six months after the date of the Signature by the Ministers Plenipotentiary or Sooner if possible.

In faith whereof the respective Plenipotentiaries have Signed these articles in the French and English languages; declaring nevertheless that the present Treaty was originally agreed to in the French language; and have thereunto affixed their Seals.

Done at Paris the tenth day of Floreal in the eleventh year of the French Republic; and the 30th of April 1803.

> Robt R Livingston [seal]
> Jas. Monroe [seal]
> Barbé Marbois [seal]

Page 39: Meriwether Lewis's Journal Entry of February 24, 1806, Describing the Eulachon, or Candlefish

Transcription

…and the mouth opens to great extent, folding like that of the Herring. it has no teeth. The abdomen is obtuse and smooth, in this differing from the herring, shad, anchovey &c. of the Malacapterygious order and clafs [class] clupea, to which however I think it more nearly allyed [allied] than to any other altho' it has not their accute and serrate abdomen and the under jaw exceeding the upper. the scales of this little fish are so small and thin that without manute [minute] inspection you would suppose they had none. they are filled with roes of a pure white colour and have scercely [scarcely] any perceptable [perceptible] alimentary duct. I found them best when cooked in Indian stile, which is by rosting [roasting] a number of them together on a wooden spit without any previous preperation whatever. they are so fat that they require no aditional sauce, and I think them superior to any fish I ever tasted, even more delicate and lussious [luscious] than the white fish of the Lakes which have heretofore formed my standard of excellence among the fishes. I have herd the fresh anchovey much extoll'd but I hope I shall be pardoned for believing this quite as good. the bones are so soft and fine they form no obstruction in eating this fish.

LOSSARY

colony A territory that is geographically far from the country that governs it.

duty A tax paid on goods brought into or taken out of a country.

empire A group of countries, territories, or colonies placed under a single government or ruler.

envoy A government official who is sent on diplomatic missions to another country.

expedition A journey undertaken by a group of people for a specific purpose.

Hidatsa Plains Indian allies of the Mandans, another Plains tribe.

journal A written record of contemporary events and observations.

keelboat A long bargelike riverboat, used on the Mississippi and Missouri Rivers for travel or shipping goods.

Mandan Plains Indians of the upper Missouri who lived in villages, hunted buffalo, and farmed the land.

pirogue An open canoe-like boat, with or without a sail.

Plains Indians Native American people of the Great Plains.

port A city with a harbor where ships can anchor and load and unload passengers and goods.

prairie Rich, lush grassland of the lower Missouri.

ratify To formally approve or confirm.

Shoshone A large group of Native Americans living west of the Rockies. They were hunter-gatherers.

treaty A formal agreement or pact between countries.

transaction An exchange of goods, services, or money.

FOR MORE INFORMATION

Historic New Orleans Collection
Williams Research Center
410 Chartres Street
New Orleans, LA 70130
(504) 598-7171
Web site: http://www.hnoc.org

Lewis and Clark Center
701 Riverside Drive
St. Charles, MO 63301
(636) 947-3199

Lewis and Clark Trail Heritage Foundation, Inc.
P.O. Box 3434
Great Falls, MT 59403

Louisiana Historical Society
William D. Reeves Ph. D., President
5801 St. Charles Avenue
New Orleans, LA 70115
(504) 866-3049

Louisiana Purchase Bicentennial Commemoration
Arkansas Secretary of State's Office
Room 22, State Capitol
Little Rock, AR 72201
(501) 682-3472

Louisiana State Museum Historical Center
P.O. Box 2448
751 Chartres Street
New Orleans, LA 70176-2448
(504) 568-8214

The National Archives and Records Administration
8601 Adelphi Road
College Park, MD 20740-6001
86-NARA-NARA (866-272-6272)

National Louisiana Purchase Bicentennial Committee
313 Marillac Hall
8001 Natural Bridge Road
St. Louis, MO 63121-4400
(314) 516-6884

Web Sites

Due to the changing nature of Internet links, the Rosen Publishing Group, Inc., has developed an online list of Web sites related to the subject of this book. This site is updated regularly. Please use this link to access the list:

http://www.rosenlinks.com/psah/lopu

# FOR FURTHER READING

Ambrose, Stephen E. *Lewis & Clark: Voyage of Discovery*. New York: National Geographic Society, 2002.

Corrick, James A. *The Louisiana Purchase*. San Diego: Lucent Books, 2001.

Edwards, Judith. *Lewis and Clark's Journey of Discovery*. Berkeley Heights, NJ: Enslow Publishers, 1999.

Gaines, Ann Graham. *The Louisiana Purchase in American History.* Berkeley Heights, NJ: Enslow Publishers, 2000.

Isaacs, Sally Senzell. *America in the Time of Lewis and Clark*. Des Plaines, IL: Henemann Library, 1998.

Jaffe, Elizabeth D. *The Louisiana Purchase*. Mankato, MN: Bridgestone Books, 2002.

Rodriguez, Junius P., ed. *The Louisiana Purchase: An Encyclopedia*. Santa Barbara, CA: ABC-CLIO, 2002.

Sakurai, Gail. *The Louisiana Purchase*. New York: Children's Press, 1998.

# BIBLIOGRAPHY

Blumberg, Rhoda. *What's the Deal? Jefferson, Napoleon, and the Louisiana Purchase*. Washington, DC: National Geographic Society, 1998.

"A Brief History of Louisiana Under 10 Flags." Louisiana Secretary of State, 2002. Retrieved December 2002 (http://www.sec.state.la.us/around/brief/brief-1.htm).

Duncan, Dayton, and Ken Burns. *Lewis and Clark: The Journey of the Corps of Discovery*. New York: Alfred Knopf, 1997.

Faber, Harold. *Lewis and Clark: From Ocean to Ocean*. Tarrytown, NY: Benchmark Books, 2002.

Gold, Susan Dudley. *Land Pacts*. New York: Twenty-First Century Books, 1997.

Government Reprints Press. *State Papers and Correspondence Bearing Upon the Purchase of the Territory of Louisiana*. Washington, DC: Government Reprints Press, 2001.

Hotchner, A. E. *The Louisiana Purchase*. St. Louis, MO: Virginia Publishing Co., 1997.

Kastor, Peter J. *The Louisiana Purchase: Emergence of an American Nation*. Washington, DC: CQ Press, 2002.

Kroll, Steven. *Lewis and Clark: Explorers of the American West*. New York: Holiday House, 1995.

"Louisiana Purchase Bicentennial." National Louisiana Purchase Bicentennial Committee, 2002. Retrieved December 2002 (http://www.umsl.edu/~loupurch/index.html).

Sprague, Marshall. *So Vast So Beautiful a Land: Louisiana and the Purchase*. Athens, OH: Swallow Press, 1991.

Tallant, Robert. *The Louisiana Purchase*. New York: Random House, 1952.

PRIMARY SOURCE IMAGE LIST

Page 5: An 1803 map entitled "A Map of North America," by John Luffman. Courtesy of the Geography and Maps Division of the Library of Congress.

Page 9: An 1868 print entitled *De Soto's Discovery of the Mississippi in 1541* by William Henry Powell. Housed in the New York Public Library. Courtesy of Art Resource, NY.

Page 11: A 1718 engraving by H. Bridgman of Jean Baptiste Le Moyne, Sieur de Bienville. Courtesy of the Hulton Archive.

Page 13 (left): A portrait of Charles III by Francisco de Goya y Lucientes. Housed in the Museo di S. Martino, Naples, Italy. Courtesy of Scala/Art Resource, NY.

Page 13 (right): A 1748 portrait of Louis XV by Maurice-Quentin de La Tour. Housed in the Louvre, Paris, France. Courtesy of Giraudon/Art Resource, NY.

Page 16: A 1784 engraving depicting the British surrender at Yorktown entitled *Reddition de l'Armée du Lord Cornwallis* by Jean Jacques François Lebarbier. Engraved by François Godefroy. Courtesy of the Hulton Archive.

Page 19: An 1805 portrait of Thomas Jefferson by Rembrandt Peale. Courtesy of Bettman/Corbis.

Page 22: A portrait entitled *Napoleon in His Coronation Robes* by François Gerard. Housed in the Chateaux de Versailles. Courtesy of Giraudon/Art Resource, NY.

Page 24: A 1764 map entitled "Plan de la Nouvelle Orleans" by Jacques Nicolas Bellin. Housed in the Louisiana State Museum.

Page 27 (top left): A c. 1800 copper engraving of Robert R. Livingston based on a portrait by John Vanderlyn Courtesy of the Hulton Archive.

Page 27 (bottom right): A copper engraving portrait of James Monroe based upon a c. 1861 painting by Alonzo Chappel. Courtesy of the Hulton Archive.

Page 30: A c. 1804 political cartoon entitled "The Prairie Dog" by James Akin. Courtesy of the Hulton Archive.

Page 32 (top): Napoléon Bonaparte's authorization for the purchase of Louisiana by the United States, dated April 30, 1803 (ink on vellum). Housed in the New York Historical Society. Courtesy of the Bridgeman Art Library.

Page 32 (bottom): A print created by Andre Castaigne entitled *Bonaparte Discussing the Louisiana Purchase Treaty with Talleyrand and Marbois*. Printed by H. Davidson. Housed in the Historic New Orleans Collection. Courtesy of Louisiana State University.

Page 34 (top left): The Louisiana Purchase Treaty, dated April 30, 1803, signed in Paris by Robert Livingston, James Monroe, and François Barbé-Marbois. Housed in the National Archives.

Page 34 (inset): Cover of Section III of the Louisiana Purchase Treaty signed in Paris on April 30, 1803. Housed in the National Archives.

Page 37 (top left): An 1807 portrait of William Clark by Charles Willson Peale. Courtesy of Independence National Historic Park in Philadelphia, Pennsylvania.

Page 37 (bottom right): An 1807 portrait of Meriwether Lewis by Charles Willson Peale. Courtesy of Independence National Historical Park in Philadelphia, Pennsylvania.

Page 39: A page from Meriwether Lewis's journal, dated February 24, 1806, and including a sketch and description of a eulachon, or candlefish. Housed in the Missouri Historical Society Archives.

Page 41: A painting by Ed Fisher entitled *Lewis and Clark at St. Charles, May 21, 1804*. Commissioned in 1989 by the Missouri Banker's Association. Housed in the Missouri State Archives Building in Jefferson City, Missouri.

Page 43: William Clark's October 1805 sketch of the Great Falls of the Columbia River. Housed in the Missouri Historical Society Archives.

Page 46 (top): A wood engraving entitled *Mandan Village Around a Sacred Ark*, c. 1830. Courtesy of North Wind Picture Archives.

Page 46 (inset): An 1832 oil painting entitled *Four Bears, Second Chief in Mourning (Mandan)* by George Catlin. Housed in the Smithsonian American Art Museum.

Page 49: (top) A map entitled "A Map of Lewis and Clark's Track Across the Western Portion of North America From the Mississippi to the Pacific Ocean," c. 1806, by William Clark. Courtesy of the American Philosophical Society.

Page 52: An 1859 map entitled "Map of the United States and Mexico" by Johnson & Browning. Housed in the Humanities and Social Sciences Library, Map Division, of the New York Public Library.

INDEX

About the Author

Jan Goldberg is an experienced educator and the author of more than thirty-five nonfiction books and hundreds of educational articles, textbooks, and other projects.

Photo Credits

Front cover, back cover (middle right) Louisiana State Museum, Gift of Dr. and Mrs. E. Ralph Lupin; back cover (top left and bottom right) Library of Congress Prints and Photographs Division; back cover (top right) National Park Service, artist, Keith Rocco; back cover (middle left) Yale Collection of Western Americana, Beinecke Rare Book and Manuscript Library; back cover (bottom left) Woolaroc Museum, Bartlesville, Oklahoma; p. 1 © Bettmann/Corbis; pp. 5, 49 (top) Library of Congress Geography and Map Division; p. 9 The New York Public Library/Art Resource, NY; pp. 11, 16, 27, 30 © Hulton/Archive/ Getty Images; p. 13 (left) Scala/Art Resource; pp. 13 (right), 22 Réunion des Musées Nationaux/Art Resource, NY; p. 19 Collection of The New-York Historical Society; p. 24 Louisiana State Museum, Gift of the Friends of the Cabildo; p. 32 (top) New-York Historical Society, New York/Bridgeman Art Library; p. 32 (bottom) The Historic New Orleans Collection; p. 34 National Archives and Records Administration; p. 37 Independence National Historical Park; p. 39 American Philosophical Society; p. 41 Lewis and Clark, 1804 by L. Edward Fisher, Missouri Bankers Association; p. 43 © National Geographic Image Collection; pp. 46 (top), 49 (bottom) © North Wind Picture Archives; p. 46 (bottom) Smithsonian American Art Museum, Washington, D.C./Art Resource, NY; p. 52 Map Division, The New York Public Library, Astor, Lenox, and Tilden Foundations.

Designer: Nelson Sa; Photo Researcher: Cindy Reiman